W9-ACC-717

A Listen to
Patriotic Music

Written by
Sneed B. Collard III

Rourke
Educational Media

rourkeeducationalmedia.com

www.rourkeeducationalmedia.com

PHOTO CREDITS: Cover: © sjlocke (drums), © Mark Coffey (trumpet), © silvanoo audisioo (guitar/sheet music), © Diana Walters (flag); page 4: © Doug Schneider; page 5: © Heidi Marie Rice; page 6: © Jacom Stephens; page 8: © GYI NSEA; page 9: © Wikipedia, © Yarinca; pages 10, 11, 12, 13, 15, 16, 17, 18: courtesy Library of Congress; page 13: courtesy U.S. Navy; page 18: © Associated Press; page 19: gary718; page 20: © instamatics; page 21: © Brandon Alms; page 22: © Neil Sullivan, © Tim Mosenfelder

Edited by Precious McKenzie

Cover and Interior design by Tara Raymo

Library of Congress PCN Data

A Listen to Patriotic Music / Sneed B. Collard III
(Art and Music)
ISBN 978-1-62169-881-4 (hard cover)
ISBN 978-1-62169-776-3 (soft cover)
ISBN 978-1-62169-981-1 (e-Book)
Library of Congress Control Number: 2013936790

Rourke Educational Media
Printed in the United States of America,
North Mankato, Minnesota

Also Available as:

ROURKE'S
e-Books

Rourke
Educational Media

rourkeeducationalmedia.com

customerservice@rourkeeducationalmedia.com • PO Box 643328 Vero Beach, Florida 32964

TABLE OF CONTENTS

What is Patriotic Music?

Music plays a role in all of our lives. We dance to it. We work to it. It can make us laugh, or cry, or think.

But one kind of music does more than that. It helps us feel love for the nation we live in. This kind of music is called **patriotic music**.

Every country has music with special meaning to its people. Have you ever watched the Olympic Games? Whenever a country's **national anthem** is played, people from that country proudly stand at attention.

But what makes a piece of music patriotic?

Just hearing The Star-Spangled Banner *makes Americans want to stand and put our hands over our hearts.*

Most patriotic music arises from a major event in a nation's history. Hail to the Chief, *for example, is the song played when the U.S. President makes an appearance. It became popular after the War of 1812.*

The words and **melody** of patriotic songs help people feel proud of their country, military, and leaders. Patriotic songs make people feel they belong in their country and have important roles to play.

To learn more about patriotic music, let's take a closer look at some of America's most important patriotic songs.

The patriotic song *Yankee Doodle* became popular during the American Revolution. No one is sure who wrote it. The melody of the song was popular by 1767, several years before the Revolution. Over time, many authors changed and added lyrics, including the line about macaroni!

Our National Anthem

The Star-Spangled Banner is based on a poem by a lawyer named Francis Scott Key. During the War of 1812, the **British** burned our capital city, Washington, D.C. Soon, the British attacked Fort McHenry, which protected the nearby city of Baltimore.

Francis Scott Key watched British ships fire cannons at Fort McHenry all night long. The next morning, Key was amazed to see an American flag still flying over the fort! Key felt so moved by the sight that he scribbled down a poem on the back of an envelope.

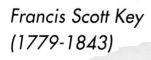

Francis Scott Key (1779-1843)

The Star-Spangled Banner isn't just the name of a song. It is also the name of the flag that flew over Fort McHenry. The flag now hangs in the Smithsonian National Museum of American History in Washington, D.C.

Like most patriotic songs, *The Star-Spangled Banner* was set to a tune that was already popular. Americans didn't seem to mind. *The Star-Spangled Banner* soon became a favorite patriotic song.

Herbert Hoover
(1874-1964)

On March 3, 1931, President Herbert Hoover signed a law making The Star-Spangled Banner *the official national anthem of the United States of America.*

Military bands play it during flag ceremonies. It is sung at World Series baseball games.

The melody for *The Star-Spangled Banner* was based on a song called "*The Anacreontic Song*". Believe it or not, this song came from Great Britain, our enemy during the War of 1812!

The Civil War

The **Civil War** divided and shaped our country in ways that we still feel today. It's no surprise that the war gave rise to dozens of patriotic songs. Two of these are especially important: *Dixie* and *The Battle Hymn of the Republic*.

Dixie was actually written before the Civil War began. It became popular all over America. Once the war started, the song became a symbol for the South, the states that wanted to break away from the rest of the United States.

Civil War State Map
(1864)

■ Union States (North)
■ Union Territories without Slavery
■ Union Territories with Slavery
□ Border Union States
■ Confederate States (South)

The Battle Hymn of the Republic was also based on a song written before the war. Northern soldiers began making up their own **lyrics** to go with a tune called *John Brown's Body*. Finally, Julia Ward Howe wrote her own patriotic lyrics. During the Civil War, the tune served as an anthem for the North, or northern states.

Julia Ward Howe
(1819-1910)

Did you know that the "northern song" *The Battle Hymn of the Republic* was based on a song by a Southerner, William Steffe? The "southern song" *Dixie* was based on a song by a Northerner named Daniel Decatur Emmett!

John Philip Sousa

John Philip Sousa
(1854-1932)

If you've ever been to a 4th of July concert, you've heard a tune by John Philip Sousa. Known as "The March King", Sousa was born in Washington, D.C. in 1854. He began working for the United States Marine Band at age 13. By 1880, he was in charge of the band.

Sousa wrote hundreds of musical pieces, but he is best known for his patriotic marches. Every 4th of July, his song *The Stars and Stripes Forever* is played across the country, including at our nation's capital.

A Patriotic Vision

Not all patriotic music comes from wars and the military. *America the Beautiful* celebrates all that is good about our nation. Katharine Lee Bates penned the words after climbing Colorado's Pike's Peak in 1893. With words such as "amber waves of grain," "purple mountain majesties," "brotherhood," and "liberty," she shared her love of the country.

A church organist named Samuel A. Ward wrote the music. The result is a song that still stirs the hearts of Americans.

In the song America the Beautiful, Pike's Peak was the inspiration for the line "purple mountain majesties."

Patriotic Music: Past, Present, and Future

Many kinds of patriotic music have been written: band marches, folk songs, classical music, country music, and even rock and roll. Musicians still write patriotic music today. Will these patriotic songs be celebrated years from now? Only time will tell.

In *Where Were You When the World Stopped Turning*, country singer Alan Jackson talked about healing after the September 11th terrorist attacks. In *Born in the U.S.A.*, rocker Bruce Springsteen reminds us that all Americans deserve equal opportunities to succeed in life.

Glossary

British (BRI-tish): people from Great Britain, the countries of England, Ireland, Scotland, and Wales

Civil War (SI-vul WORE): the war to keep the United States as one country when certain states tried to form their own country

lyrics (LEER-iks): the words of a song

melody (MEL-oh-dee): the instrumental music or tune of a song

national anthem (NA-shun-ul AN-thum): the official song or tune of a country

patriotic music (PAY-tree-AW-tuk MEW-zik): music that reflects the pride and love for a nation

Index

Websites

www.amhistory.si.edu/starspangledbanner

www.folkways.si.edu/explore_folkways/radio.asp

www.scoutsongs.com/categories/patriotic-songs.html

About the Author

Sneed B. Collard III has written more than 65 books for young people including the award-winning books *Animal Dads*, *Shep—Our Most Loyal Dog*, and *Teeth*. His popular mysteries *The Governor's Dog is Missing* and *Hangman's Gold* feature history of the Old West, not to mention the popular 4th of July music *The 1812 Overture*. Learn more about him at www.sneedbcollardiii.com.

Meet The Author!
www.meetREMauthors.com